MW01504556

# The Road of Leadership

**Stephen R. Gaines, FACHE**

The Road of Leadership, © 2010 by Stephen R. Gaines
The Gaines Group; Houston, Texas

ISBN-13: 978-14563539-3-3

ISBN-10: 14563539-3-4

Category: Leadership and Business Management

The Road of Leadership
Written by Stephen R Gaines, FACHE
www.leadershipessentials.co

Published by The Gaines Group
Houston, Texas
©2010

# Table of Contents

Preface                                                    13

Introduction                                               17

Chapter 1: Definition of Leadership                        21

Chapter 2: Leadership Essentials                           31

Chapter 3: Servant Leader                                  41

Chapter 4: Roles of Leadership                             51

Chapter 5: Tear Down the Walls                             63

Chapter 6: Customer-Based Organizations                    73

Chapter 7: Leadership Styles                               89

Chapter 8: Leader vs Manager                              107

Chapter 9: Steve's Hints for Leaders                      117

Appendix A: The Leader's Checklist                        131

Appendix B: Leadership for the Small World                139

*In addition to the many people who inspire me*

*to pursue my journey of leadership*

*in my professional life,*

*this book is dedicated to*

*Laura, Stephanie and Emily who inspire me*

*to pursue my journey of leadership*

*in my family life.*


*Thank you all*

*and I wish you safe travels on*

*The Road of Leadership.*


*I hope you enjoy ... srg*

*November 2010*

# The Road of Leadership

# Preface

After almost 30 years of experience in leadership roles with half of that time spent training and coaching future leaders, I felt compelled to write *The Road of Leadership* using academic theories and personal experiences as my guide.

There are literally hundreds of books on the market about leadership and just as many opinions of how it should be done. Fortunes have been made by many on the lessons of leadership. However, the simple fact is; what works for some may not work for others and vice versa.

The keys to being an effective leader are: keep it simple; keep it real; relate to the people; earn trust and credibility; make solid decisions and stick with them; share successes; and, accept responsibility.

Leadership is a learned skill. Leaders are made; not born. Leadership is an art; not a science. Leaders have different methods and possess different traits and characteristics. Some leaders are better than others in given situations.

After reading and studying this book will you be a great leader? Maybe, but it takes a lot of work and a lot of dedication. This book will explain the fundamentals and roles of leadership and give you the tools to apply them.

This book is structured with an Author's Note and Discussion Exercise after each Chapter. The Author's Notes are personal reflections of the text material and the Discussion Exercises are designed to assist you in applying the material to your daily life of leadership.

The demands of Leadership and the demands on Leadership are ever-changing. Given the current social and financial circumstances in the world, these demands may have never been greater. Current leaders are under great pressure to perform and the next generation of leaders is sure to face situations that prior generations never did; hence the need for leaders to be proactive, involved and knowledgeable of their market.

I have truly enjoyed my experiences in leadership. To be completely honest, most of the fun has been watching those around me grow in their own life of leadership. I hope that some of my influence helped in their transitions but, the truth is, they each possessed great potential and were eager to learn. Given those factors, my part was easy.

I hope this book assists you in your pursuit of leadership and I hope you enjoy *The Road of Leadership*.

*Stephen R. Gaines*

# Introduction

In today's climate of ever-changing and competitive markets, economic woes and increasing customer needs, the demand for leadership is arguably at an all-time high regardless of the business type. Whether it is Healthcare, Logistics, Manufacturing, Communications or Merchandising, each business type needs strong and proactive leadership to minimize negatively impacting unforeseen events.

In recent years, the advances in communication, marketing and information sharing have progressed almost beyond anyone's imagination. Twenty five years ago if you had described today's digital world, electronic communication and electronic business environment to a stranger on the street as the normal state of affairs they would have urged you to seek psychological counseling. But, look around. The world has changed and it has changed quickly.

Leadership is no different. Leaders of organizations must keep abreast of their market environment or they will most assuredly fall behind or worse, cease to exist. Leadership is a multi-layered skill consisting of many traits and characteristics. The role model leader must be proficient in all of them.

This text will discuss the definition of leadership, the character and traits required for leadership and, perhaps most importantly, the role and commitments of the leader.

Leadership is not easy and at times can be a very lonely career choice. That is why so few actually reach it and maintain it for long periods of time. If you are in a leadership role remind yourself regularly that leadership is an art and not a science. There is no wonder drug that will magically cure all ailments and no mathematical formula to find the correct answer for each decision. Rarely will you make a decision that you do not later replay in your mind and wonder if it was the right one.

Note the title of this text; Road OF Leadership as opposed to Road TO Leadership. This is important to note as leadership is a continuous journey and not a resting place. You cannot become stagnant in leadership skills nor business skills. Stagnation in leadership and business equates to death in leadership and business.

I hope you enjoy the words and ideas on these pages and I hope you find it helpful in your own leadership journey.

I wish you safe travels on the Road of Leadership.

# Chapter

# - 1 -

## Definition of Leadership

What is Leadership?

If you asked a hundred people on the street you would probably get a hundred different responses, even from those that function as leaders.

The dictionary defines leadership as: *the function of a leader; the ability to lead; the act of guiding or directing; the leaders of a group.* A leader is defined as:

*one that leads, guides or directs.* The root word of leadership and leader is of course "lead" which is defined as: *to go before others to show the way; and to influence or guide in direction.*

If you are reading this text it is assumed you are either interested in exploring the notion of becoming a leader or you are a current leader that perhaps wants to brush up on your skills. If you are the prior do you have what it takes to lead dozens perhaps hundreds or thousands of individuals with individual characteristics and traits? Are you willing to trust others with your organization's fate? If you are the latter, are you performing as a leader in the definitive sense of the word? Are you actually guiding the people of your organization through processes on a daily basis?

It is a given that the leader is the one who guides and directs or perhaps goes in front to show the way to others. Is this true in today's business world? Do all leaders actually lead the way as defined? Do you see leaders of top organizations out on the street paving the way for their team?  The answer is more than likely not very often, if ever.

For this text, research on the definition of leadership from prominent leaders and organizations was gathered and studied.  The definition varies somewhat between individuals and organizations but this can be accounted for by the environmental and social challenges over time.  For instance, the leadership skills required during the first decade of the 1900s are quite different from those required for the first decade of the 2000s.  A century in which technological advances occurred faster than any other made a huge difference in the required leadership skills.

Rarely recognized is the need for leadership skills to be fluid and flexible and available at a moment's notice. No better example exists than the leadership skills required in the twentieth century.

Studying the twentieth century as a whole, there were two World Wars; wars in Korea, Vietnam and Middle East; the Great Depression; arguably at least two recessions; political and social changes including the Civil Rights movement, Voting Rights and The New Deal; and the multitude of advances in technology, business and communications.

The twentieth century was a unique time in American History. The demand for leadership skills of the government, military and corporate leaders was immense at times and had to be accessible within a short timeframe.

Interestingly, the United States Army's definition of leadership has evolved through the years. In 1948 leadership was defined as *"the art of influencing human behavior through ability to directly influence people and direct them toward a specific goal."* In 1961 leadership was defined as *"the art of influencing and directing men in such a way as to obtain their willing obedience, confidence, respect and loyal cooperation in order to accomplish the mission."* In 1993 leadership was defined as *"the process of influencing others to accomplish the mission by providing purpose, direction and motivation."*

The United States Air Force's definition of leadership has remained constant through the years and states *"leadership is the art of influencing and directing people to accomplish the mission."* The subsequent text of Air Force Leadership states *"the basic concept the effective leader must keep in mind encompasses two fundamental elements; the mission and the people."*

Rudy Giuliani, the former mayor of New York City from 1993 through the terrorist attacks on the World Trade Center in 2001, described leadership thusly. *"There are many qualities that make a great leader. But having strong beliefs, being able to stick with them through popular and unpopular times, is the most important characteristic of a great leader. Leaders need to be optimists. Their vision is beyond the present."*

Jeff Immelt, the CEO of General Electric was interviewed by Fast Company in 2004 and, at that time, expressed his *"10 Things Leaders Do: 1) personal responsibility, 2) simplify constantly, 3) understand breadth, depth, and context, 4) the importance of alignment and time management, 5) leaders learn constantly and also have to learn how to teach, 6) stay true to your own style, 7) manage by setting boundaries with freedom in the middle, 8) stay disciplined and detailed, 9) leave a few things unsaid, and 10) like people."*

Through the years the definition of leadership has evolved and most certainly will continue to evolve. This is normal because the demands of leadership change. The world changes and therefore leadership styles, traits, character and abilities need to change and adapt to the changes. The requirements of leaders in today's environment are much different than the requirements of leaders 50-100 years ago.

As will be discussed later in the text, leaders must keep abreast and continue to evolve with their markets. "Status quo" does not last long in the business and leadership world.

## *Author's Note:*

I recently had the pleasure of attending a gathering with Jeff Immelt, CEO of General Electric, and James Baker, chief of staff and treasury secretary for President Ronald Reagan and secretary of state for President George H.W. Bush.

Jeff Immelt discussed the traits he considers to be the keys to good leadership in today's environment. It was interesting to hear thoughts from the perspective of the leader of one of the largest corporations in the world as GE operates businesses in aviation, healthcare capital equipment and software, financing, appliances, oil and gas, wind energy and many more.

The keys for an effective leader are: adaptability to markets, networking, simplicity in communicating complex issues, being proactive, ability to do analytics quickly, systems thinking, understanding globalized markets, planning, negotiating, optimism and genuineness, a true set of core beliefs and instilling pride and confidence in those you lead.

As I review this list of "competencies" of an effective leader, I myself wonder how one person can fulfill these requirements. And, fact is, they are requirements in today's environments. Leading a corporation as large and globally positioned as General Electric, as well as many others of similar structure, could be an overwhelming task for one person to handle alone.

These attributes are not just necessary for a large company such as GE but they are necessary in today's business environment for companies of any size. Today's leader must be flexible, versatile and extremely knowledgeable of their own market.

I'll touch on this later in the text but an effective leader MUST have a strong team around them. An effective leader MUST trust the people to complete the tasks given to them. An effective leader MUST delegate appropriately. An effective leader MUST keep their fingers on the pulse of the organization and, most importantly, an effective leader MUST maintain credibility.

## *Discussion Exercise:*

At your next staff meeting ask your employees to look around the room and identify the leader of your organization, department, division, etc. More than likely they all will point back at you.

However, if you are an effective leader and demonstrate the majority of these characteristics in your life of leadership, the answer you should receive will be *everyone in the room.*

**_Reader's Notes_:**

simple
real
relate to people
earn trust and credibility

# Chapter

# - 2 -

# Leadership Essentials

Effective leaders possess certain characteristics which are essential in their life of leadership. The list of possible characteristics is endless because of the almost infinite situations in which leaders may find themselves. This text will discuss what is viewed as the essential characteristics or traits that an effective leader must possess.

The United States Air Force lists six traits which are considered to be vital in their leadership model. These traits are *integrity, loyalty, commitment, energy, decisiveness and selflessness.*

The United States Marine Corps lists 14 leadership traits which are considered qualities of thought and action and help earn the respect, confidence and loyal cooperation of other Marines. They are *justice, judgment, dependability, initiative, decisiveness, tact, integrity, enthusiasm, bearing, unselfishness, courage, knowledge, loyalty and endurance.*

Henry Kissinger, author, foreign policy expert and 56th Secretary of State, stated, *the task of the leader is to get his people from where they are to where they have not been.*

Kissinger's statement can be linked to the basic definitions of leadership; *lead the way and provide guidance and a vision.*

The sixth President of the United States, John Quincy Adams, stated *if your actions inspire others to dream more, learn more, do more and become more, you are a leader.*

John Quincy Adams served as President of the United States from 1825-1829 and was the son of John Adams, the second President. Even at that time in history only 50 years after the beginning of the United States as we know it, being inspirational was understood to be a basic fundamental of leadership.

Winston Churchill served as Prime Minister of Great Britain during World War II between 1940 and 1945. His leadership traits included *integrity, energy, self-belief, vision and decisiveness.*

In *The Leadership Challenge* James Kouzes and Barry Posner identify five fundamentals of leadership. They are *challenge, inspire, enable, model and encourage.*

These fundamentals can be translated for the leader as the following: *Challenge* the workforce to accomplish goals; lead them in an *Inspirational* manner instead of one of punishment and force; *Enable* them by providing the necessary tools to accomplish goals; be a role *Model* to others; and *Encourage* them through the process by instilling confidence. All of these fundamentals are required of the leader when empowering the workforce.

James Collins, author of "Good to Great" and "Built to Last" included *display high levels of persistence, overcome significant obstacles, attract dedicated people, influence people toward achievable goals and guide the company through crucial episodes* in his description of leadership.

*To increase the standard of living and the quality of life for all stakeholders* is the Basic Task of Leadership according to Stephen Covey, author of "The 7 Habits of Highly Effective People" and "The 8th Habit".

Think about that for a moment.  The basic task of leadership, according to Covey, is to improve the life of all the stakeholders which includes employees, customers, business owners and stockholders if applicable.  This is a large task for a leader and one that cannot be taken lightly.

Max Weber, a German sociologist of the late 1800s, said *institutions that endure thrive not because of one leader's charisma but because they cultivate leadership throughout the system.*

Weber stated this phrase over one hundred years ago and how true it is even today.  Cultivating leadership is essential to the success and endurance of any organization.  Cultivating, in the farming sense of the word, is the churning, tilling and refining of the soil during the planting season.

An effective leader understands that a succession planning program is vital for an organization to endure.  A succession planning program includes identifying prospective leaders and continuously challenging them progressively until they are ready to assume higher level responsibilities.

The timeframe of the aforementioned quotes ranges over one hundred years and come from different individuals. Even so, there is a common theme between them. Leaders build self-confidence in others by challenging, inspiring and encouraging personal growth. They believe in their own abilities and are role models to others.

Effective leaders will take risks and venture outside of their comfort zone. This behavior is an inherent trait of an effective leader as they want to create something new. Leaders desire to make something happen and will not settle or be satisfied with status quo.

Leadership is a two-way conversation; a dialogue not a monologue. Understanding this component is key for an effective leader. The leader must understand the needs of employees and the employees must have an understanding of the leader in order for the tasks and goals to be accomplished.

Leaders also understand the need of employee ownership. Through empowerment, appropriate delegation, instilling confidence and encouragement in the workforce, an effective leader will transform their staff from being simply employees to being interested parties in the success of the business; owners. They will then legitimately care about how it performs operationally and financially.

## *Author's Note:*

Much like a cake needs milk, flour, eggs, flavoring and heat to be a cake, a person needs the fundamentals, necessities or essentials to be a leader. Without all of these ingredients, no one is completely capable of performing as an effective leader.

These essentials are so important that I named the leadership training arm of The Gaines Group "Leadership Essentials".

It is true the list of essentials may be endless given the circumstance but there are similarities between them all. Remember, leadership is a multi-skilled art and the leader must have a mix of knowledge, experience and, sometimes, luck to accomplish all the tasks.

## *Discussion Exercise:*

If you have not already done so, ask your employees to list the top 5 to 10 traits they would like to see in their leaders.

This will be valuable information for you to identify the traits and the type of leader that the employees desire and perhaps the answers will reveal the traits that are missing from the current leadership.

## *Reader's Notes*:

# Chapter

# - 3 -

## Servant Leader

The portrayal of the servant leader dates back to Biblical times. The management philosophy of "Servant Leadership" or "Servant Leader" entered the corporate world when Robert K. Greenleaf wrote his 1970 essay titled *The Servant as Leader*. In that essay he said;

> *"The servant leader is servant first. It begins with the natural feeling that one wants to serve, to serve first. Then conscious choice brings one to aspire to lead. That person is sharply different*

*from one who is leader first, perhaps because of the need to assuage an unusual power drive or to acquire material possessions. The leader first and the servant first are two extreme types. Between them there are shadings and blends that are part of the infinite variety of human nature."*

So what does this mean to us in the leadership field? If we want to become servant leaders, are we to only focus on the needs and desires of our employees; those we lead? Not necessarily, however, we must know and understand those we lead and we must empathize with those we lead.

A basic principle to remember and practice in a leadership role is: *without employees a leader is alone and without a leader the employees have no guidance or direction.* Understanding this relationship dynamic is the key to leadership success.

The fact is leadership and employees need each other in order to accomplish tasks and goals. Neither can survive without the other so a positive relationship must exist for best results.

Figure 10.1 is a traditional style organizational chart demonstrating the leader of the organization at the top with direct and indirect reports linked below. If we were to request the organizational charts from leading organizations around the world, probably 99.9% of them would return to us a chart of similar appearance.

**Figure 10.1**

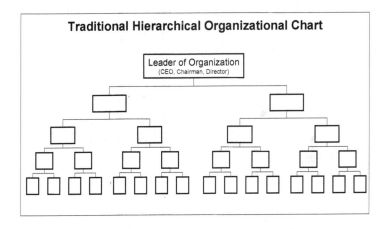

The physical characteristics of the figure symbolically implies that information and decisions are made at the top of the organization and all else rolls down the chain. However, Figure 10.2 demonstrates the organizational structure of a Servant Leader environment. The difference is obvious. The chart has been turned upside-down with the leader now at the bottom.

**Figure 10.2**

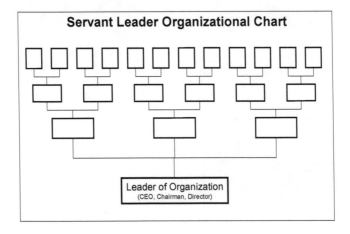

Does this structure imply that the leader of the organization takes orders from everyone else? No; not at all. It simply signifies the empowerment placed on the front-line workers and that the leader is accountable and responsible to others in the organization.

Obviously, the leader of the organization, the CEO or the President, is ultimately responsible for everything that happens within a corporation operationally and financially. However, a servant leader understands the importance of the employees and will place the employees' needs above their own.

## *Author's Note:*

Recently I gave a leadership-related lecture to a group of healthcare leaders at the Medical Center in Houston, Texas.  During the lecture I began describing the servant leader environment and I said, "Picture in your mind the traditional pyramid-shaped organizational chart.  What happens when you turn the traditional structure upside-down?"

A voice from the crowd said, "It rests on a single point – a single person – and it becomes unsteady."

If I were to take a pyramid shaped object made of glass or plastic which was resting on a table and flip it over to try to balance it on its point, of course it would topple over.     But, this is untrue of the servant leader organizational structure.

In a servant leader organizational structure the model actually becomes stronger because there are more people responsible and accountable for the interests and success of the company.  The front-line staff becomes empowered to make decisions thereby instilling confidence and ownership in them and the leader functions as the support system of the structure.

## *Discussion Exercise:*

Imagine this scenario:

You have learned your skills through a mix of education and experience. You have opened a new business and your product is Leadership. Your employees are your customers and they are solely responsible for your success.

Recognizing the dependence on your employees for your own success, describe how you would manage and care for them in this scenario. And, would your behaviors and interactions differ from your current methods?

## Reader's Notes:

WHAT DOES THE
STAFF NEED TO BE
SUCCESSFUL?

# Chapter

# - 4 -

# The Roles of Leadership

A leader wears many hats and no single label can describe the roles a leader assumes on a daily basis. This should be no surprise in today's globalization and competitive markets.

Some of the roles a leader may assume are Coach, Salesman, Cheerleader, Psychologist, Actor, Player, Motivator, Mediator, Negotiator and Soothsayer; just to name a few.

In addition to all of these roles perhaps the most important is that leaders manage change and provide direction. It is impossible for one person to solely change an organization. It requires the input and efforts of many. The leader provides the impetus for change; sets the direction and manages the hurdles throughout the process.

Without the leader identifying the initial reason for change and providing the continued momentum to move the process along, the change would not take place or would cease to exist soon after its inception. People are inherently resistant to change so a leader must constantly monitor progress and continue motivation until it is completed.

Even though an effective leader wears many hats there are a few basic roles that every leader has in common. A few of these are discussed below.

### *1. A Leader leads.*

Leaders do many things but their primary responsibility is to lead others to work toward a common goal or purpose. They also motivate, inspire and influence in the process.

### *2. A Leader influences beyond their scope.*

Leaders see the "big picture". Therefore they must be able to look outside of their normal boundaries to influence change.

This characteristic is especially important within a boundaryless organization where completely separate functions must interact with each other and function as one. Having an across-the-board understanding and the ability to interact and motivate business functions outside their normal realm is a key function of an effective leader.

### *3. A Leader leads by example.*

Leaders are role models for others. They are the example for others to follow. Leaders must maintain standards and demonstrate effective behaviors.

## 4. A Leader communicates.

Leaders communicate in dialogue; not monologue. They understand the importance of listening to others; especially those that offer ideas for positive change.

Effective leaders realize communication is one of their most powerful tools and allow it to flow freely throughout the organization.

## 5. A Leader creates a positive environment.

Leaders are responsible for establishing and maintaining an environment conducive to learning and positive expectations and attitudes.

## 6. A Leader knows their personal attributes.

An effective leader must know their own personal attributes including strengths and weaknesses. To take this notion a step further, an effective leader should realize their opportunities and threats to personal success.

Businesses examine their Strengths, Weaknesses, Opportunities and Threats (SWOT) routinely, especially when entering new markets. A leader should also do a

SWOT-like self-analysis on a regular basis in order to make sure they are prepared for change and aware of their markets; see Author's Note.

### 7. A Leader develops and educates others.

Succession planning is a key part of an effective leader's function. To ensure a good plan, leaders encourage and support the growth of individuals by mentoring them to assume higher level positions.

### 8. A Leader develops a team.

Leaders realize they cannot accomplish all tasks alone therefore they must surround themselves with knowledgeable people to form a team. The leader then sets the goals and direction for the team and trusts them to complete the task at hand.

An organization will suffer if all members were to act individually without direction. Leaders should have a good understanding of how the various functions of operations interact when developing their teams to get the most out of them.

### 9. A Leader gets results.

Leaders are judged by their accomplishments and we learned earlier in the text that leaders strive to accomplish great things. Therefore, leaders should provide guidance, develop trustful teams and manage resources to accomplish tasks.

### 10. A Leader accepts responsibility.

Leaders are responsible for fulfilling the organization's mission. With this comes the acceptance and giving of praise when things go well and the acceptance of the consequences when things go bad.

The 33rd President of the United States, Harry S. Truman, had a sign on his Oval Office desk which read *The Buck Stops Here*. This quote symbolized that he was ultimately in charge and took full responsibility for all decisions. Incidentally, President Truman gave the approval to drop two atomic bombs on Japan on August 6 and 9, 1945. Japan surrendered five days later.

## _Author's Note:_

One of my favorite exercises to do during my leadership lectures is to ask the attendees what they consider to be the roles of leadership and how they describe their own role.

A few terms regularly offered are coach, salesman, mentor and friend, as well as many others.

I agree with all of these roles except friend.

A leader can be empathetic and understanding of their employees but there is a fine line between empathy and understanding and being a friend.

When the line of friendship is crossed, the ability to remain non-biased in the areas of favoritism, discipline enforcement and credibility becomes questionable.

Another exercise I like to do when working with leadership groups is to have each person do a self-reflective analysis. An exercise which comes to mind is the SWOT analysis that is typically performed by businesses entering a new market or performed by businesses in rebuild mode. A SWOT-type analysis is beneficial for leaders as well.

For an individual's use, I have revised the commercial business SWOT by replacing "Opportunities" with "Ambitions" and Threats can be described as Hindrances which may block the success of the leader. Hence, we then have SWAT. Having an understanding of one's own Strengths, Weaknesses, Ambitions and Threats is essential to an effective leader.

## *Discussion Exercise:*

Reflect on your career and list the leaders that have had influence over you; good and bad.

Decide if they were able to regularly fulfill the roles of leadership or sometimes missed the mark. Chances are in your experiences with good leaders they will have fulfilled most or all of the roles. Try your best to be non-biased in your account of the bad leadership experiences.

Figure 4.1 is a SWAT template. As an exercise, list the Strengths that make you an effective leader; list your Weaknesses as you see them; list your Ambitions and; list the Threats or Hindrances you see that might be in your way to becoming a better leader.

**Figure 4.1**

| STRENGTHS | WEAKNESSES |
|---|---|
| AMBITIONS | THREATS |

## *Reader's Notes*:

# Chapter

# - 5 -

## Tear Down the Walls

Tear down the walls. Boot out bureaucracy. Open the doors. Eliminate internal boundaries that hinder progress. Alert the neighbors and let the sun shine in. Create synergy among your business functions and use it to the fullest.

Does this sound refreshing? If you are currently in a bureaucratic driven organization where timelines are measured in years, it is as refreshing as a cold glass of tea *(or insert favorite beverage here)* on a hot summer day.

Nothing can annoy an effective, proactive leader more than the inability to accomplish necessary changes in a timely manner.    Lack of communication and cooperation between independent business groups can stifle an organization and be detrimental to its long-term success.

Figure 5.1 depicts the silo mentality.   Notice the people joined together in groups and the groups separated from the others.  The term *silo organization* describes an organizational structure in which there is no or limited communication between business functions.

**Figure 5.1**

Figure 5.2 is a simple diagram of a silo organization which includes Operations, Marketing, Human Resources and Finance.    Typically in a silo organization these business functions will have their own leader and will function independently with little regard for the mission and efforts of the others; a standalone business.

**Figure 5.2**

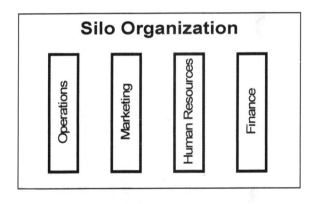

Jack Welch, former CEO of General Electric, coined the phrase *"boundaryless organization"* when he wanted to revamp the way the company did business within their organizational structure. At the time GE had several businesses under the main umbrella, as they still do today, which functioned as independent organizations. There was very little, if any, crosstalk or use of synergy between them. This scenario frustrated Jack so he implemented the boundaryless environment and the rest is history.

Figure 5.3 demonstrates a boundaryless organization in which there is interaction between business functions. This interaction creates synergy among the functions which fosters coordinated efforts to meet the organizations goals as a whole.

**Figure 5.3**

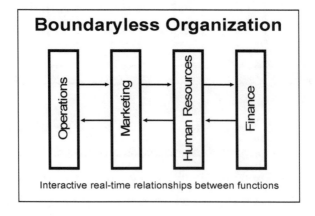

### *Synergetic Environment*

A synergetic environment occurs when the boundaryless organization is taken to the next level. Figure 5.4 depicts the organizational structure and the bi-directional arrows demonstrate the lines of communication.

**Figure 5.4**

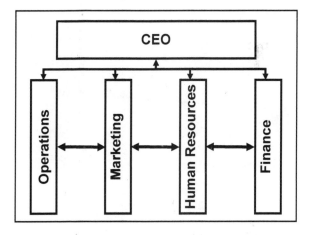

Not only do all of the business groups horizontally communicate in the synergetic environment there is also upward and downward communication. With an environment of open communication between all business groups and upper level management they become one. Synergy among all participants is created and the business groups function and accomplish goals as a unit instead of independent standalone businesses.

## *Author's Note:*

I start each of my lectures to management and leadership groups in the same manner. Once all of the house rules are explained and out of the way the attendees are instructed to remove their name tags and place them face down on the table. Completely removing them and placing them in purses or briefcases is an even better idea. I then explain that they are now in a TFZ; a Title Free Zone where all comments, all attendees and all ideas are given equal opportunity for evaluation.

By doing this, a boundaryless or synergetic environment has just been created in the conference room; a great first step toward the goal.

Try this step at the beginning of your next staff meeting. If attendees are given equal time to speak you may be surprised at the results and new ideas that are shared.

## *Discussion Exercise:*

If you suspect inefficiencies or frustrations among your workforce, meet with the front-line employees and ask them to identify the hindrances that prohibit efficiency. More often than not issues beyond their control will be identified.

Since management tends to see issues from their own perspective, it is best to not include them in these meetings. You should reserve this time to interview front-line employees only. They are the ones closest to the problems and issues and they will most likely give the best solutions.

If you are a leader that is somewhat removed or does not have a good understanding of daily operations, it is also a good idea to have an operations-type person attend as well. However, this person should not be involved in the daily management of the area of focus.

## *Reader's Notes*:

# Chapter

# - 6 -

# Customer-Based Organizations

What is a Customer-Based Organization?

A Customer-Based Organization (CBO) is one that has matured to the point of focusing on the needs and desires of its customers. A CBO has all infrastructures in place including lines of communication, operations, processes, leadership and possesses adequate resources which allow flexibility in the market.

## *Characteristics of a CBO*

CBOs are typically mature organizations in that they have had time to develop the infrastructural details as opposed to newly-formed or young organizations. Additionally, CBOs have been in business long enough to become familiar with their customer market and their customers' needs. Communication flow within the CBO is the most important component as explained later in the text.

Examples of CBOs are General Electric, Apple and Dell. Each of these organizations has experience in their market and has shown the ability to be flexible based on market needs. General Electric was formed in 1892 when Edison Light and Thomson-Houston merged. Apple was formed in 1976 by Steve Jobs and Steve Wozniak and soon after delivered the first Apple I personal computer. Michael Dell formed Dell Computer Corporation in 1984 with $1000 and an idea of direct marketing of computers. The single similarity in each of these organizations is the mission of knowing their customers, knowing what their customers want and having the flexibility and resources to meet the desires; thereby making them a Customer-Based Organization.

## *The Wagon Wheel Organizational Chart*

So far in this book several types of organizational structures have been discussed; traditional, servant, silo, boundaryless and synergetic.   When considering the unique market position and functions of a CBO the best characterization of its structure is the Wagon Wheel Organizational Chart; Figure 6.1.

**Figure 6.1**

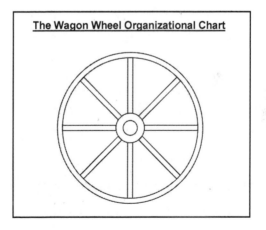

The Wagon Wheel Organizational Chart

## *Components of the Wagon Wheel*

The Wagon Wheel Organizational Chart consists of the outer rim, the spokes, the cog and the spaces between the spokes; Figure 6.2.

**Figure 6.2**

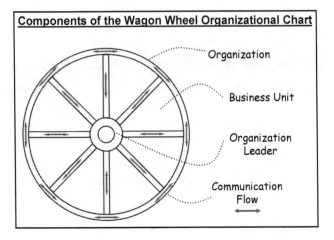

The outer rim and spokes of the wheel represent the channels of Communication, the cog of the wheel represents the Leader of the organization and the spaces between the spokes represent each Business Units.

## Communication in the Wheel

Communication in the CBO is the foundation of its success. It must flow freely and in all directions; up, down and across each Business Unit. As compared to the communication flow of Boundaryless Organizations, the CBO's environment has a more open communication environment at all levels.

In a CBO where the focus is on the customer, the CBO will typically have developed a formalized customer-group or user-group in which feedback and comments from the customers are directly filtered back to the appropriate division of the CBO. This feedback is digested and used for product development, product enhancements or any operational changes deemed necessary.

Using Apple as an example, the online Apple User Group is an international database of millions of Apple users and customers of all ages and expertise. Within this group, the members can ask questions and make comments regarding computer system operations, shortcuts, product information and so forth. Chances are a member of the group will have an answer to any question asked by other members. If not, there is a mechanism within the user group to ask a question of Apple engineers and technicians and, most often, their answers are posted to the group.

In effect, Apple understood the needs of their customers and met them by creating an online support department with relatively low cost associated as it is staffed by fellow customer users. This is a great example of customer communication.

Figure 6.3 demonstrates the communication flow in the Wagon Wheel. Communication in the Wagon Wheel flows in all directions and includes customers, business units and the leaders.

**Figure 6.3**

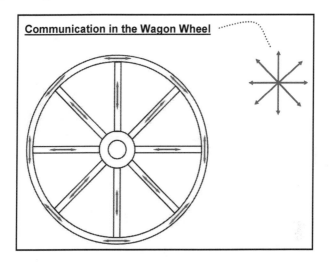

*The Business Units*

The Business Units or Divisions of the organization are characterized as the pie-shaped spaces between the spokes. The Business Units consist of the leadership of the unit, the operations and processes components and, most importantly for the CBO, the customers. Figure 6.4 provides detail of the Business Unit structure.

**Figure 6.4**

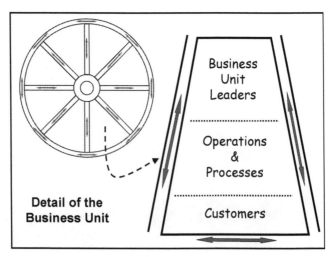

The Business Unit realizes its existence is based upon the satisfaction of meeting the customers' needs. Therefore, the customer is the foundation of each Business Unit and communication flows up and down from customers to leaders as well as to the other Business Units.

## *Effects of a Broken Spoke*

Just as a well-maintained spoke supports the integrity of an actual wagon wheel, so does it support the organization.  Thereby, a broken spoke weakens a wagon wheel as it will weaken an organization.

In the Wagon Wheel Organizational Chart the spokes represent the flow of communication in the CBO.  With communication being the primary component of success to the CBO, any hindrance to its smooth flow must be corrected quickly.

## *Leaders of a Customer-Based Organization*

Leaders of CBOs must possess self-confidence, excellent communication skills and open-mindedness.

As we have learned, CBOs focus on the needs and desires of their customers.  Given this, a CBO leader actually gives up a portion of control to the customers, hence, the need to be self-confident and open-minded.

Processes and functions such as Product Development and Service Support are somewhat dictated by the customer's needs and adjusted according to the customers' feedback. This component is the essence of the CBO's success.

Does this imply the organization is run by customers; of course not. Organizations will always need infrastructure; leaders, management, supervision, and front-line workers. However, the CBO goes the extra mile by considering their customers as part of their team.

*Author's Note:*

For years I've studied organizational structures and their effectiveness. In my opinion, I've considered the Boundaryless environment developed by Jack Welch to be the best and have tried to emulate it throughout my career in various organizations. However, after much thought of how to improve the Boundaryless environment, I developed the term *Customer-Based Organization* and demonstrate its structure with the *Wagon Wheel Organizational Chart.*

The Customer-Based Organization performs like Boundaryless on steroids. Communication flows real-time in all directions across the internal structure of the organization as well as to and from the customers. The customers' needs and desires are the focus of the CBO and taken into account prior to setting the direction of the organization.

In today's economic environment, the need for customer satisfaction and understanding and meeting their demands is at an all-time high. If all points are performed correctly, the CBO has a better chance of success than any other type of organization. After all, customers are the lifeline of all organizations. If the customer is kept happy and feels a sense of ownership they will keep coming back.

With the help of my consulting team members, I recently implemented the CBO environment in a hospital system in the Texas Medical Center in Houston. The system consists of several hospitals and a dozen or more satellite centers spread throughout the community.

The system was a prime candidate for a CBO transition as each of its locations functioned independently. Sharing of information was non-existent; customer satisfaction was relatively low; and services and leadership functions were duplicated throughout the locations driving up costs. Customers were experiencing lengthy waits for appointments and, once in the system, they were not happy with the service received.

Given the rules and regulations of the healthcare business, the initial focus was to have a similar infrastructure for each location while consolidating leadership in the areas which made sense. Once the new leadership and management structure was in place and functioning to an appropriate level, we began revising those Policies and Procedures that could be shared among all of the facilities. We then reviewed front-line staffing models; highlighting excess and opportunities to share staff between locations.

Remember from the text that CBOs are mature organizations and unless adequate infrastructure is in place a CBO transition will fail. The initial infrastructure-building steps were necessary for this hospital project and, depending on the amount of infrastructure necessary, some delays may occur during your own CBO transition.

Once the infrastructure was in place, we could then focus on the needs and desires of the customers. We already knew that getting an appointment in the system was difficult. We found the appointment schedule restrictive, inconvenient to customers and unfriendly to flexibility. Simply by expanding the appointment schedule to include evening and weekend appointments we immediately established a CBO.

By implementing these changes, customer satisfaction went up and volume and revenue went up to record levels. Making the transition even more impressive was the fact that no capital costs were incurred; only additional labor costs which were miniscule compared to the new revenue.

The results of implementing a CBO environment can be amazing. I hope you can use the information from this chapter to develop your own CBO.

My plan is to dedicate a follow-up book to *The Road of Leadership* with additional information about CBO environments and to include more case studies involving CBO transitions.

## *Discussion Exercise:*

1. Would you define your current organization as Customer-Based?

2. If not, what would it take to implement the CBO environment?

3. Transpose your current organizational chart into a Wagon Wheel Organizational Chart.

4. Identify areas of concern and any "broken spokes" that might hinder the implementation of a CBO environment.

*Reader's Notes:*

# Chapter

# - 7 -

# Leadership Styles

If you are reading this book more than likely you have interviewed for a management or leadership position at some point in your career and at least one of the interview questions pertained to your leadership style.    It is probably the most popular and enduring question at management and leadership interviews.

It is important for a leader to know their preferred leadership style, but to also understand there is no single style that covers every situation. Different situations require different styles.

In this text several leadership styles and traits will be discussed. It is the responsibility of the leader to understand these and know how to appropriately apply each.

## TRADITIONAL LEADERSHIP STYLES

There are three traditional leadership styles; Laissez Faire, Participative and Autocratic.

### *Laissez Faire Leadership Style*

Laissez Faire is primarily a "hands off-anything goes" leadership style. This style works well in an environment of highly trained, disciplined and focused self-directed employees; employees that need little to no supervision. Given this, the Laissez Faire leadership style is rarely effective in large organizations in which there are multiple levels of various functions and personalities.

## Autocratic Leadership Style

The Autocratic style is one of complete control by management; micro-management. This style is not very popular among leaders of large organizations primarily because it is logistically impossible for a leader to control all aspects of a large organization. The autocratic style has lost favor through the years as employee satisfaction and retention has become a strong focus. However, an autocratic style is appropriate during emergent situations and can be used as a temporary style when a commanding approach is necessary to gain control.

## Participative Leadership Style

The Participative style, which is similar to the Democratic style, is highly popular among large organizations. It is a hybrid of Laissez Faire and Autocratic and allows the leader to move from one style to the other depending on the immediate situation.

Employee participation in decision-making is a component of the Participative style but not to the degree of the Democratic style. With the Participative style, the leader retains the right for final approval of decisions whereas the Democratic style allows decisions to be made by consensus.

Table 7.1 is a quick reference of the traditional leadership styles.

**Table 7.1**

## Traditional Leadership Styles

- **Laissez Faire** – little management control; self-directed employees

- **Autocratic** – high level of management control; no input from employees

- **Participative** – moderate management control; some input from employees

## MODERN LEADERSHIP STYLES

In recent years, research of the effects of management has grown and several new leadership styles have emerged. These include Situational and Transformational leadership.

### *Situational Leadership Style*

Situational leadership, a product of management theory research by Ohio State University and the University of Michigan in the 1950s, maintains there is no single leadership style for all situations. Leaders must be flexible and adjust their leadership style according to the situation at hand.

Paul Hersey and Kenneth Blanchard of *The One Minute Manager* fame developed a Situational Leadership model which included four traits; Telling, Selling, Participating and Delegating.

The Telling leadership trait consists of one-way communication from the leader to the workforce. The leader defines the roles and what, when and how the tasks will be performed. This style is most effective when the workforce has low levels of readiness and maturity.

The Selling leadership trait consists of two-way communication to achieve buy-in from the workforce. This style is used when the leader needs to influence others; as in selling their vision and ideas.

The Participating leadership trait describes the sharing of decision-making between the workforce and leadership with the primary role of leadership being facilitator and communicator. This style is used when employee buy-in and consensus is necessary to gain results.

The Delegating leadership trait describes an environment of parceling out orders and tasks to the workforce. This style is used when the workforce is mature and ready to accept additional responsibilities and should be viewed as a reward for good management of prior duties.

Table 7.2 summarizes the traits identified by Hersey's and Blanchard's Situational Leadership model.

**Table 7.2**

## Hersey and Blanchard Traits

- Telling: one-way communication, leader defines roles and task methods

- Selling: influencing of workforce necessary

- Participating: consensus and buy-in of workforce

- Delegating: assignment of additional responsibilities to workforce

Daniel Goleman, author of *Emotional Intelligence* and *Primal Leadership*, related the importance of applying Emotional Intelligence to the role of a leader. He discussed that a leader should be capable of recognizing the emotional traits of others in order to motivate and manage them to the fullest of their ability.

He identified six styles that effective leaders should switch between given the situation. These are: Visionary, Coaching, Affiliative, Democratic, Pacesetting and Commanding.

The Visionary leadership style is considered to be the most effective and one of inspiration. The visionary leader provides their ideas or vision of the organization in its future state to the workforce but does not set the rules as to how to accomplish it. The visionary leader inspires the workforce and allows others to chart the path to reach the goal.

The Coaching leadership style is perhaps the least used of them all since it tends to consume a lot of a manager's time. Coaching is a one-on-one style that focuses on the personal development of the employee rather than the process of completing tasks. Coaching consists of building a personal relationship and trust between the employee and manager thereby making the employee more receptive to the coach's recommendations.

The Affiliative leadership style is one in which the leader recognizes the employees as people and acknowledges the emotions of the employees. This style is best used when increasing morale and repairing broken trust in the organization. However, exercise caution when using it. Too much focus on the emotions of the employees may lead to bias and hinder the leader's ability to discipline poor performance.

The Democratic leadership style, sometimes referred to as the Participative style, is one of consensus-building; seeking and implementing the ideas of employees by majority. This style can be a great motivation tool. However, it should be used with caution as it is capable of leading to endless meetings, disagreements and disaster should the information from incompetent employees be acted upon.

The Pacesetting leadership style is an "entrepreneurial-type" style that works well with a workforce of highly motivated, highly competent employees which have a common goal. Given this type of workforce, a leader can set the direction and target and allow the workforce the freedom to accomplish. Most often, goals are not only met prior to the deadline but will exceed expectations.

The Commanding leadership style, also referred to as the Authoritative or Coercive style, is one that should be used only on occasion and reserved for emergent situations in which complete control is necessary. This "do as I say" style was common in the military and the early beginnings of the corporate world but is somewhat frowned upon in today's management environment. Widespread use of the Commanding style can lead to poor employee morale, high turnover and ultimately poor organizational performance overall.

Table 7.3 summarizes the leadership traits developed by Daniel Goleman.

**Table 7.3**

| Leadership Traits Identified by Goleman |
| --- |
| • Visionary: provides "big picture" ideas but not how to accomplish |
| • Coaching: time-consuming, builds coach-employee relationship |
| • Affiliative: recognizes and supports emotions of employees |
| • Democratic: consensus building |
| • Pacesetting: entrepreneurial; highly motivated and competent workforce |
| • Commanding: top-down direction; "do as I say" |

## *Transformational Leadership Style*

The Transformational style is all about making change happen throughout the organization. In order for this style to work effectively a leader must possess a mix of the aforementioned traits for different types of situations.

Leading an organization through a transformation or turnaround, a leader will initially provide their futuristic view of the organization demonstrating the Visionary trait. The leader must then obtain buy-in from the stakeholders including employees, management and board members, if applicable, demonstrating the Selling trait. Once the vision has been "sold" to the stakeholders, the leader will the provide direction and guidance while using a mix of the other traits to complete the transformation.

## *Author's Note:*

After reading this chapter do you feel overwhelmed by the number of different traits and styles a leader should possess and, after taking inventory of your own traits, perhaps somewhat inadequate?

If you are like most people, you answered yes. Worry not because you are in the same boat with the best of leaders.

Leadership is a tough career choice. Not only must a leader wear a number of hats they must also possess the traits listed in this chapter. It is no wonder only a select group of people make it to top leadership positions and maintain them.

My research of the Top 500 global corporations revealed that in 2008, 37% of North American CEOs left their positions versus 28% in the prior year and the average tenure of a North American CEO was 6.8 years as compared to 8.6 years in the prior year.

As a comparison of the same period, Europe's rate of CEO departures was 32% and Asia Pacific's was 24%. The average tenure of a CEO in Asia Pacific increased to 5.7 years from 4.3 years and the CEO tenure in Europe remained constant.

There is no doubt that the demands and expectations of leadership are great and, depending on the type of business, these grow exponentially. High pressure environments such as Healthcare and Finance are likely to experience shorter tenures of leadership ranging from 2 to 4 years primarily due to the demand and expectations of high performance.

My prior publications include textbooks on the subject of Healthcare, Human Resources and Healthcare Finance. From personal experience, the pressure of decreased reimbursements and ever-increasing regulations of the federal government, play a tremendous role in the sliding tenure of healthcare executives.

Healthcare is a uniquely complicated financial environment and I'll attempt to summarize it in this manner.

In the normal world of the consumer/provider relationship, a consumer rarely if ever receives a service or a good without knowing the cost prior to purchase. And, rarely in the normal world of the consumer/provider relationship do consumers pay different, sometimes drastically different, prices for the same service or good. However, in the healthcare environment, this is the normal routine and it happens thousands of times every day.

There are a multitude of reasons for this scenario which include:

- pricing scales based on reimbursement from government payors (Medicare, Medicaid and Children's Insurance Plans);
- contracted pricing agreements which may include decreased charges to certain demographics based on volume received by the

provider (private insurance company agreements);

- consideration for the percentage of indigent population a particular healthcare system provides when calculating reimbursement (Disproportionate Share and Upper Payment Limits programs).

Does the healthcare financial environment sound complicated? The financial environment alone is enough to drive a healthcare leader insane. Additionally the pressures of hiring and, more importantly, retaining highly educated and highly paid individuals to work in the system contribute to the relatively short tenure of healthcare leadership.

I referenced healthcare in this chapter's Author's Note only because it is the environment in which I am most familiar. However, all businesses have their unique challenges for leadership; whether it is shortage of supply and workforce which cause delays in product delivery or challenges in receiving adequate financing to expand services. When things go wrong who gets the blame?

## *Discussion Exercise:*

1. List the leadership styles and traits that you have exhibited over the past 6 months.

2. Review your list and decide if the styles and traits you exhibited were the correct choices for each situation.

3. Whatever your type of business, list the challenges that face your leaders on a daily basis. In your opinion, do these challenges affect the longevity of leadership and why?

4. If applicable, think back over time and list the people that have been in the primary leadership roles in your organization. How long did they remain in that position? Does this answer reveal anything about the longevity of leadership in your industry?

## *Reader's Notes:*

# Chapter

# - 8 -

## Leader vs. Manager

Is there a difference between leading and managing?  The simple answer is *yes*.

This is not to imply that managers do not play a role in leadership or are not capable of leading.  Indeed they are.  However, for the purpose of this text, the terms leader and manager will be viewed as they exist in the corporate or business structure and how they relate to a corporate or business workforce.

Leaders set the direction for the organization and provide guidance. They encourage and inspire the workforce and, since they have the vision of the organization in its future state, leaders are typically responsible for long-range and strategic planning. Leaders also seek and create growth opportunities for the organization and thereby create opportunities for the workforce.

Managers perform the day-to-day operations of organizing the workforce and carrying out the vision of the leader. They are the "local" expert and answer questions of their immediate workforce. Managers focus on their primary responsibilities within the organization.

Peter F. Drucker, teacher, author and consultant who modernized management theory, wrote *management is doing things right; leadership is doing the right things.*

Stephen R. Covey, author and management consultant, wrote *management is efficiency in climbing the ladder of success; leadership determines whether the ladder is leaning against the right wall.*

Table 8.1 serves as a quick-reference guide for the functions of leaders and managers.

**Table 8.1**

| Leader versus Manager | |
|---|---|
| Leaders: | Managers: |
| • Set direction | • Perform day-to-day operations |
| • Provide guidance | • Carry out the vision |
| • Strategize | • Make sure things are done correctly |
| • Plan long-term | • Enforce policy |
| • Provide vision | • Instruct and coordinate workforce |
| • Encourage | |
| • Mentor | |
| • Inspire | |

An alternative way to view the difference between leaders and managers is that leaders manage ideas and visions while managers manage process and people. Leaders have followers. Managers have subordinates and they are subordinates themselves.

Leaders are responsible for the entire organization from top to bottom and every aspect in between. Managers are responsible for the performance and outcomes of their individual pieces of the organization.

### *The Manager to Leader Transition*

The focus of this book is on leadership; its fundamentals, roles, styles and so forth.  But, since leaders are "made" and not "born", where do they come from?

Can a manager transition to a leader?  Yes, with support from the leaders they follow and hard work on their own behalf.

At some point in their careers, all leaders held entry level positions and eventually moved to management positions in which they were responsible for the performance of a particular business focus and workforce; a wheel spoke.  Given the average age of a CEO is 57; it is unlikely that a person begins their career as a leader of an organization.

Through mentoring, knowledge and charisma a manager can transition to a leader. A manager has a much better chance of transitioning to a leader when paired with a successful and experienced mentor. An experienced mentor is invaluable as they act as a guide through unexpected difficulties. An effective leader possesses a broad understanding and knowledge of their business. A manager must acquire a high level of knowledge of the business prior to becoming leader. Perhaps the most overlooked trait of a leader is charisma; the magnetic charm that arouses loyalty or appeal; the "it" factor. A leader must have charisma to win over supporters and to be able to communicate to vast numbers of people.

## *The Failed Manager to Leader Transition*

Even though the Manager to Leader transition is possible through mentoring, training, charisma and hard work, the success of the transition is not guaranteed. Reasons for failure vary but the primary reasons are immaturity, inability to relate to the "big picture", lack of knowledge and charisma.

Immaturity as a reason for the transition failure does not imply the manager-to-leader is young in age or emotionally undeveloped. It describes their immaturity in their role; their position; their job. Most often this scenario is seen when the manager-to-leader is promoted up through the ranks too quickly and has not had ample time to gain experience in vastly different situations.

The inability to see the "big picture" is detrimental to a manager-to-leader. This hindrance signifies the manager-to-leader is unable to break the cultural mold of management and therefore will maintain "tunnel vision". Using the wagon wheel as a mental image, the manager-to-leader is unable to think outside of their spoke and therefore has difficulty understanding and relating to the other divisions of the organization.

The lack of knowledge and charisma also hinders the success of the manager to leader transition. An effective leader must have an understanding of all of the organizations operations. Otherwise, respect and loyalty of the employees will be difficult to obtain.

## *Author's Note:*

Have you ever worked for someone that occupied a leader role but that person never quite broke out of the manager mentality?    How frustrating and de-motivating this scenario can be; especially if you possess leadership skills.

Having lived through this scenario myself and having experienced de-motivation and frustration to the max, I can offer a bit of advice.

Mentoring and educating followers are components of being a leader and, given that you possess leadership skills, you could try performing these functions in reverse mode.

## *Discussion Exercise:*

1. Summarize the duties of your managers and make sure they fit into the defined role of a manager.

2. Identify managers which demonstrate a hybrid of manager and leader traits.

3. Develop a plan of how you would transition those managers from Manager to Leader.

## *Reader's Notes:*

# Chapter

# - 9 -

# Steve's Hints for Leaders

This chapter is an addendum to Chapter Four; *The Roles of Leadership*. Chapter Four was originally titled *The Commandments of Leadership* but it felt sacrilegious to have my own commandments so I re-titled it and added my *Hints for Leaders*.

The Hints obviously are not commandments but are a less formal instruction or directive that can guide you in your daily life of leadership. Each is of equal importance so they are not listed in any type of hierarchy.

## *HINT # 1:*
## *Build a confident workforce*

Confidence is the belief in one self and throughout this book empowering others has been discussed as one of a leader's major roles. Empowering the workforce and instilling confidence in them go hand in hand and only by doing can confidence be acquired.

## *HINT # 2:*
## *Do not micromanage*

A leader's responsibility is to see the "big picture" and NOT to manage every detail of every situation. Inspire others to get the job done because only by doing will others learn. In effect, by not micromanaging their workforce, a leader is empowering and instilling confidence in others.

## *HINT # 3:*
## *Seek input from front-liners*

Leaders should actively seek input from those they lead for best practices and improvements.

No one knows the processes better than those that perform them first-hand every day and the majority of the best improvement ideas will come from those closest to the problem.

Successful leaders listen to their people and are always looking for good ideas from them to act upon.

## *HINT # 4:*
## *Surround yourself with knowledgeable people and trust them to do their job*

Effective leaders surround themselves with a knowledgeable team and trust them to complete their tasks.

Trusting the people around you yields empowerment, confidence and ultimately a succession plan. All are keys to good leadership.

Leaders that are incapable of trusting others most likely possess underlying personal issues of mistrust, lack of self-confidence, immaturity in their role and other insecurities. Successful leaders know their own strengths and weaknesses and work to correct them continuously.

Theodore Roosevelt, the 26th President of the United States and the youngest man to ever hold the Office, stated *the best executive is the one who has sense enough to pick good men to do what he wants done, and self-restraint to keep from meddling with them while they do it.*

Build a strong team of great people. A leader does not have to know every detail of every process but be able to inspire others to do it.

## HINT # 5:
### *Leadership is an art; not a science*

Being an art, there is no mathematical formula to find the answer to every leadership decision. The majority of leadership decisions is different and can be vastly unique. Effective leaders possess a mix of experience and knowledge and use them in harmony to find the best solutions.

## HINT # 6:
### *Know your business and face reality*

Perform this experiment at your next staff meeting. Ask the attendees the following; "What business are we in?" It is interesting to hear the varied responses.

Then ask the group "Who are our customers?" Again, the varied responses will be interesting.

A leader should clearly communicate the focus of the business so everyone knows the answer. A leader should also clearly communicate the organization's customers. Perhaps this is best accomplished in a mission statement if the organization is of significant size.

In the customer-based organization customers exist within and outside the organizational chart. Our customers keep the doors of our businesses open and without them all businesses would fail.

## HINT # 7:
### Investigate new ideas and accept change

Today's leaders must be able to adapt to changing markets and have extensive knowledge of those markets. If a leader becomes stagnant in their approach and in their market their business will die.

## *HINT # 8:*
## *Credibility completes the leader*

The strongest mandate to leaders is to maintain your credibility.  Other functions of a leader such as mentoring, empowering and motivating can be taught but credibility is a reflection of the leaders' character and without it a leader cannot lead.  It is that simple.

Credibility is defined as trustworthiness; capable of being believed; believable; worthy of belief or confidence.  Imagine a leader that has shown they are untrustworthy or incapable of being believed.  Imagine having to question everything your leader says.  Should this occur, the bond of respect and loyalty is broken and most likely can never be repaired.

Through the years I have had the opportunity to coach leaders that had lost their credibility in one way or another.  To be perfectly honest, regaining credibility is a long uphill climb and there is no guarantee it can ever be repaired.

A leader must have the trust and complete faith from those they lead.  This includes trust in the leader's abilities and complete faith in the judgment of the leader when making decisions.  If there is the slightest doubt about either of these in the minds of the followers, a leader cannot lead.

## HINT # 9:
## Communicate complex issues in a simple manner.

Ronald Wilson Reagan, the 40th President of the United States of America earned the title as "The Great Communicator".  Not because of an eloquent style but because of the genuineness, humility and simplicity in which he communicated complex issues.

He had the ability to "connect" with his audience and was able to do it in a manner in which everyone understood the message.

Below are excerpts from his Oval Office speech regarding the Space Shuttle Challenger tragedy, his speech in West Berlin which contains probably the most memorable lines spoken during his Presidency and his Farewell Address in which he downplays the title of "Great Communicator".

*"The crew of the space shuttle Challenger honored us by the manner in which they lived their lives. We will never forget them, nor the last time we saw them, this morning, as they prepared for their journey and waved good-bye - - and "slipped the surly bonds of earth" to "touch the face of God." ... January 28, 1986*

*"General Secretary Gorbachev, if you seek peace, if you seek prosperity for the Soviet Union and Eastern Europe, if you seek liberalization: Come here to this gate! Mr. Gorbachev, open this gate! Mr. Gorbachev, tear down this wall!" ... June 12, 1987*

*"In all of that time I won a nickname, 'The Great Communicator.' But I never thought it was my style or the words I used that made a difference: It was the*

*content. I wasn't a great communicator, but I communicated great things, and they didn't spring full bloom from my brow, they came from the heart of a great nation -- from our experience, our wisdom, and our belief in principles that have guided us for two centuries."*
*... January 11, 1989*

Placing politics aside one cannot disagree that President Ronald Reagan was a great communicator. His ability to deliver difficult messages to millions of people in a simple and humble manner was amazing. Every leader can learn communication skills from his example.

### HINT # 10:
### Practice empathy and realize your decisions impact others

Although Leadership has its challenges it can be a fun and rewarding career choice. Sure, some days are better than others and there will be days when you question your own abilities. However, other than parenting, no other career choice offers opportunities to mentor others; grow and shape organizations and impact the lives of employees and their families.

Impacting the lives of employees and their families is a responsibility which is most often overlooked by leaders.  However, a mature, effective and empathetic leader realizes their decisions not only impact the organization but also its employees and their families.

Next time you face a major decision or consider reducing your workforce, take time to realize how the decision will impact others.

## *HINT # 11:*
### *Keep moving on the Road of Leadership*

Note the title of this book, *The Road OF Leadership* as opposed to *The Road TO Leadership*.

Leadership is a journey and not a resting place. It is an ever-evolving art and not a science. There is no mathematical formula to solve all issues and problems.

Leadership requires judgment, character and knowledge as basic requirements. It is sometimes a lonely career choice and one of constant decision-making.

Leaders must keep abreast of their own industry and keep abreast of changes and advances within their marketplace. Stagnation or "status quo" in leadership equates to death in leadership. Hence, keep moving on the Road of Leadership.

# Appendix

# - A -

## The Leader's Checklist

What does it take to be a leader?

Appendix I is a list of some of the most popular identifiable and tangible qualities, attributes and traits of the best leaders. Additionally listed are the Supporting Traits which, when possessed and used in harmony, make a good leader a great leader.

For example, the Coach Trait has Supporting Traits of Communicator, Emotional Intelligence, Empathy, Maturity and Mentoring. Coaching becomes much more effective when all of the Supporting Traits are used in harmony as well.

The Traits and Supporting Traits checklist can be used as a self-assessment tool to identify the traits currently possessed and those that need to be obtained.

## **TRAITS AND SUPPORTING TRAITS**

___ Charisma: ability to win over followers by stimulating their emotions.

*Supporting Traits: Visionary*

___ Coach: ability to identify other's strengths and weaknesses and relate them to career goals

*Supporting Traits: Confidence, Communicator, Emotional Intelligence, Empathy, Maturity, Mentoring*

___ Communicator: able to relay complex issues in a simple manner

*Supporting Traits: Charisma, Confidence*

___ Competence: having suitable or sufficient skill; knowledge and experience.

*Supporting Traits: Confidence, Intuitive*

\_\_\_ Conscientious: sense of duty and character; high standard of excellence and desire to excel

> *Supporting Traits: Coach, Competence, Confidence*

\_\_\_ Confidence: sure of one-self and one's own abilities; full trust and trustworthiness

> *Supporting Traits: Competence, Dominance, Emotional Stability, Maturity*

\_\_\_ Decisiveness:  confident in one's decision-making

> *Supporting Traits: Coach, Competence, Confidence, Visionary*

\_\_\_ Emotional intelligence: ability to monitor one's own and others' feelings and emotions and use this information to guide others for optimal results

> *Supporting Traits: Coach, Communicator, Empathy, Intuitive, Maturity, Salesman*

___ Emotional stability: able to tolerate frustration and stress; psychological maturity

> *Supporting Traits: Coach, Communicator, Competence, Maturity*

___ Empathy: able to put yourself in another's shoes
> *Supporting Traits: Emotional Intelligence, Intuitive, Maturity*

___ Empowering: to give power or authority to

> *Supporting Traits: Coach, Communicator, Confidence, Emotional Intelligence, Maturity, Mentoring, Visionary*

___ Enthusiasm: active; expressive; energetic; optimistic

> *Supporting Traits: Coach, Communicator, Confidence, Visionary*

___ Intuitive: trust of self when making decisions

*Supporting Traits: Competence, Confidence, Maturity*

___ Maturity: recognizing by empowering others more can be accomplished

*Supporting Traits: Coach, Emotional Stability, Mentoring*

___ Mentoring: able to guide others by referencing self experiences

*Supporting Traits: Coach, Communicator, Competence, Confidence, Emotional Intelligence, Emotional Stability*

___ Negotiator: to deal or bargain with others

*Supporting Traits: Salesman, Empathy, Communicator*

___ Salesman: ability to sell ideas to others

> *Supporting Traits: Charisma, Vision,*
> *Communicator*

___ Visionary: able to establish a futuristic image of an organization

> *Supporting Traits: Charisma, Communicator*

# Appendix

# - B -

## Leadership for the Small World

Not too long ago communication was performed by Pony Express, telegrams and smoke signals. Shopping for merchandise was done inside brick and mortar locations or by catalog mail order. A bit further into history, the world was considered to be flat and there was much anxiety when ships sailed away to find the new world.

In today's environment we have cell phones, e-mail and webcams for real-time communication and online stores and electronic bill pay systems to meet our shopping needs.  The world has truly changed in a relatively short timeframe and these changes have made our world a small one.  The "small world" effects challenge leaders every day.

The globalization of business, and almost everything else for that matter, has had a tremendous effect on leadership.  Sure, there are still "Mom & Pop Shops" out there but even most of those have some sort of global connection whether it is in the supply chain, wholesale items, machinery, etc.

Figure Appendix B.1 demonstrates several things; 1) the trended value of U.S. Imports and Exports from 1900 to 2010; 2) the effects of the recession in the 2009 and 2010 numbers; and, 3) evidence that markets have become globalized.

**Figure Appendix B.1**

| USA Export:Import Value Comparison | | |
|---|---|---|
| | **Export** | **Import** |
| 1990 | $393 Billion | $495 Billion |
| 1995 | $585 Billion | $743 Billion |
| 2000 | $782 Billion | $1.20 Trillion |
| 2005 | $901 Billion | $1.67 Trillion |
| 2006 | $1.03 Trillion | $1.85 Trillion |
| 2007 | $1.15 Trillion | $1.96 Trillion |
| 2008 | $1.29 Trillion | $2.10 Trillion |
| 2009 | $1.06 Trillion | $1.56 Trillion |
| 2010 | $1.20 Trillion | $1.80 Trillion |

As evidence that globalization of markets is occurring quickly, notice in Figure Appendix B.1 that between 1990 and 2000 Exports nearly doubled and Imports nearly tripled. Also notice that the trend continued from 2000 to 2008 but slowed in 2009 and 2010. The slowing was most likely due to the economic challenges of the time.

Many books on the global economy are available as well. The purpose of including it in this text is to make leaders aware of the globalization of markets and the need to adjust to them.

## Recommended Reading and References:

S.R. Gaines, *Swimmers, Bobbers and Sinkers*, 2010

J.E. Barbuto, Jr./D.W. Wheeler, *Becoming a Servant Leader:Do You Have What It Takes?*, 2007

U.S. Army, *Army Leadership*, 2007

J. Menkes, *Executive Intelligence*, 2005

J. Welch/S. Welch, *Winning*, 2005

J.Welch/J. Byrne, *Straight From the Gut*, 2003

J. Collins/J. Porras, *Built to Last*, 1997

J.M. Kouzes/B.Z. Posner, *The Leadership Challenge*, 1995

J.M. Kouzes/B.Z. Posner, *Credibility*, 1993

S. Covey, *The 7 Habits of Highly Effective People*, 1989

U.S. Air Force, *Air Force Leadership*, 1985

R.K. Greenleaf, *The Servant as Leader*, 1970

**Feel free to send comments or questions to:**

Stephen R. Gaines, FACHE, CRA
CEO and Founder
Leadership Essentials Consulting
e-mail: info@leadershipessentials.co
Website: www.leadershipessentials.co
The Gaines Group

**About the author:**

A consultant, national speaker and published author of textbooks and articles, he holds advanced degrees in Business and Healthcare Administration. He is a Board Certified Healthcare Executive and a Board Certified Radiology Administrator. He has also held leadership roles at three world-renown academic medical centers and has over 20 years of leadership consulting experience. As CEO and Principal Consultant for Leadership Essentials, he provides clients with lectures, seminars and one-on-one executive coaching.

You can contact Stephen R. Gaines directly at info@leadershipessentials.co

Made in the USA
Lexington, KY
19 September 2012